The Motive Behind the South Sudan Civil War

Tor Dojiok Gach

Published by:
Light Switch Press
PO Box 272847
Fort Collins, CO 80527

Contents

ACKNOWLEDGMENTS

I must first thank my family and friends who have stood behind **me** to make sure that I put my best digital foot forward at all time: Kuet Dojiok Gach, Mading Yat Bol, Mut Bayath Ruey, Tang Dong Bukjiok, and Chuol Puoch Both. I appreciated their help, criticism, and encouragement. Last, of course, an acknowledge to the people so instrumental at all levels of production as editors. I must say that any, and all errors of fact or detail in this book, of which hopefully there are not too many, fall squarely on my shoulders. This book is designed to give the reader a better understanding of what is happening in Southern Sudan.

In 2011, the South gained its independence from the tyrannical Islamic North. The peace that we had fought so hard to attain for 21 years is under threat, because the man that was chosen by the people as our new president, Salva Kiir, quickly became a tyrannical dictator. He has eliminated elections; his goons take dissenters away in the dead of the night and kill them; he ignores the constitution, the rule of law, and the parliament; and rules by fiat.

The people of the Republic of South Sudan should have the right to choose either the side of the Rebels or the tyrannical regime; to choose the God-given right to freedom, or to be under the oppression of a man addicted to power. If the people choose liberty over tyranny, and unite against it, then the dictator's regime will be torn down, and the high-ranking officials who masterminded his rise to power will be arrested.

PREFACE

This Book will genuinely highlight the main points of the causes of civil war in the Republic of South Sudan. Readers, I would like to suggest to you that when you open this book, find a quiet place to read, because there is so much valuable information about which you are to learn.

Readers, my mind was so shocked when I learned that civil war had broken out in my home country on December 15, 2013. The people of Southern Sudan, who had fought a decades-long war against the Islamic North, had now turned against one another. The president's tribe, the Dinka, exerting its political power and dominion, had turned against the tribes which they had fought together; had shed blood; and had lost family and loved ones alongside. The media, including CNN, BBC and Al-Jazeera, have described South Sudan as being "on fire".

TOR DOJIOK GACH

Walden University

PhD student of Law and Public Policy

Master Degree: Administration Justice and Security

University of Phoenix

Administration Justice and Security

Bachelor Degree: Criminal Justice
University of Nebraska at Kearney

Criminal Justice

Chapter One

THE FIRST INCIDENT IN THE NEW NATION

What caused the explosion on December 15, 2013, between the top leaders Dr. Riek Machar, the Vice President, and Salva Kiir, the President of the Republic of South Sudan? Did the politics get under their skin?

It began in the early evening hours on December 15, 2013, at the meeting of National Liberation Council at Nyakuron Center. When the stakeholders namely Dr. Riek Machar, Pagan Amun, and the late Dr. John Garang's wife Rebecca Nyandeng were vetoed boycott the meeting when the President Salva Kiir used unappropriated language which brought more attention among the political rulers in the country. As attention continues mounting on the same night of December 15, 2013, President Salva Kiir had called his right-hand man, commander of the Presidential guard, Marial Cienoung of the Tiger Battalion, to disarm all the Nuer who were carrying guns present at times. A Nuer soldier who was nearby at a military equipment depot. One Nuer soldier was questioned by the Dinka soldiers and calling of name Nuer soldier (Nyegaat), meaning thief. The argument among the uniform men caused a fistfight which later become a huge impact throughout the country. Meanwhile, the two continue fist fighting, one soldier ran on to his gun, AK-47, loaded with ammunition and pointing it to the Nuer soldier, killing him on the spot. When uniformed men heard a gun shoot, they turned guns on themselves based on their ethnic groups.   Moreover, in the same evening, the situation becomes increasingly tense as Marial Cienuong, the commander of the Tiger Battalion, ordered Dinka soldiers to open the armory and distributed them to the ethnic

Dinka. Then the fighting erupted within the Presidential guards in the military barracks at Jebel, near Nyakuron Center, and continued into the next day. The fighting spread through the nearby military barracks Bilpam and Newsite. The Nuer soldiers captured military Barracks until the next day. Mr. James Hoth Mai, who was the army Chief of Staff at the time, called for reinforcements to take back the barracks. The few Nuer soldiers who controlled the military barracks were called to withdraw because they are few in number and could not keep up to fight more resistance army because there was no backup.

On the next day of December 16, 2013, Dr. Machar, the Vice President in the country, flees Juba to Jonglei for security reason because of President Kiir's plot to kill him. Dr. Machar made the right choice to save his life. Mr. Machar didn't speak until couple days later after reaching Bor town. If the government knew Dr. Machar, who is challenging him for election, I believe the President would have to go after the Vice President who fled for his life. The President of the Republic of the South Sudan had ordered his illiterate tribal militias   to search for Nuer tribes in their homes in the Nation Capital Juba. The oversight of the search was long planned by the dictator leader to sweep out the Nuer tribe's innocent young, women, and men. The question is, was he Salva Kiir who ordered his soldiers, mainly from his hometown, who go door to door killing Nuer innocent, women, men, and children. After the government knew that the killing was taking place, the President rushed to South Sudan TV accusing Dr. Riek Machar of a coup plot. The coup plot he assumed Dr. Machar has committed was not true because nowhere in the world would a human being plot a coup without an organized army. The one reason that I could think of is that Salva was to grab public attention for what happened so he can gain support from the world community.

The killings which took place in Juba on December 15, 2013, on one ethnic tribe fade up all Nuer's Generals who believed that people are one. The army generals wait patiently for the President to stop his army for killings the Nuer in State Capital. And it drained the top General Peter Gatdet who was station in Bor as Commander in Division 8th. Did in fact, announce his defection to former Vice President on December 17 and 18, 2013. On December 17 and 18, the deputy of General Peter Gatdet, from President home town, had ordered his ethnic soldiers to attack General Peter Gatdet before he decided to announce his defection against the regime. Gunfire erupted in the distance for a good few hours. General Gatdet overran Bor and rescued Dr. Machar from his way to Bor town. I believe that General Gatdet did this to rescue innocent Nuer who has been round up in their homes and massacred by Mr. Kiir's tribal soldiers. If the government didn't commit massacres of the Nuer Civilians these generals of the army from the Nuer and white army would never respond quickly to protect their people.

On December 21, 2013, as fighting continued raising to the boiling point all over the country, another top General, James Koang Chuol Ranliey, who was the commander in Division 4th of SPLA in Unity State, Bentiu did declare his defection. The well-known Major General James Koang Chuol Ranliay who was later promoted as a 1st Lt General in SPLM-IO under Commander in Chief Dr. Riek Machar. Mr. Koang Chuol then announced his loyalty to Former Vice President Dr. Riek Machar. General James Koang did not plan to defect, but he waited for Salva Kiir for six (6) days if he could make announcement to order his tribal to stop targeting the Nuer. Shortly after Mr. Kiir ordered James Koang to report to Juba or put his gun. After CDR Koang heard the order from the President, that he would need to report to army headquarters. Mr. Koang has imperially decided to make his announcement quickly dismissing all the state ministers and then became acting Governor. President and his Chief of Staff James Gathoth Mai had ordered their forces to attacked General James Koang Ranliey in Bentiu in which later repulse attackers back.

Chapter Two

THE FIGHTING INTENSIFIED SPREADING THROUGHOUT UPPER NILE STATE, MALAKAL

As the battle continues, African and other world leaders immediately move quickly calling both Dr. Machar and Salva to stop fighting and to come to the negotiation table. However, when a ceasefire was signed the negotiations mediators IGAD plus eight regional nations the Intergovernmental Authority on Development as well as the African Union, United Nation, EU, China, USA, UK, and Norway. The peace agreement treaty was signed in Ethiopia Capital Addis Ababa. The government of Ethiopia has played very abrasive roles not by standing as a double agent during the peace processing agreement. African leaders must understand that no nation is perfect, but what happened to South Sudan today, will tomorrow occur in any Africa countries. I'm referencing the involvement of Uganda army to South Sudan's internal problem. Uganda gave their support for the government and have deployed its troops to major cities in the country. The States like Malakal, Bentiu, Bor, and Juba. In protecting of the regime that has sought by slaughtering its citizens in the eyes of the International Community in daylight.

Chapter Three

CONTINUES STRUGGLE OR LEAVE IT

Nothing comes to work until you work for it and there is no question even though it could cost you when you don't look for better ways to defeat your opponents at all level. I think every citizen is responsible for what happened in the country and to stand up for what is right. Mr. Kiir would regret for the rest of his life and those who advised him to make a bad decision that he had in mind. In my mind, I believe that Kiir would one day have to be arrest and his advisors and will apologize to the People of South Sudan, even though he could not educate the public enough for the causes of the incident.

African is in deep trouble as the continent, as a whole, is mounting towards a civil war. I can see African leaders are relaxing crossing their feet on their laps while others part of the continent is on flame finishing themselves. Is this leadership we want to see as African people to kills each other over for many decades? I thought that the definition of African Union is standing for taking care of African problems which are the main subject in the continent today. Reconciliation and unity of the SPLM Government and SPLM/A-IO Pagak. The inter- South Sudan fighting and devastation caused personal losses, and now it's a great concern to the people.

Insisting on a peace agreement will also place people on the same page as president Salva Kiir's putting personal interest above suffering. The President behavior, which he doesn't accept the opinion of his people, is now opting for a military solution as the way to resolve the leadership problem.

Chapter Four

THE FIRST WORLDS COUNTRIES CAN'T BE TRUST TO HANDLES AFRICAN ISSUES

African leaders could be trusted if they could play a greater role in helping. But countries in this world have their internal problems which they would never call others world leaders to intervene in their domestic issues. As African, we must think of the way forward to take care of our concerns. I believe that our country is a country for the people who live in it. In 1983, North and South's Civil war which caused 1.9 million lives lost was the involvement of all South Sudan tribes against the Islamic North. But their participation which ends to have South Sudan as a nation would have to admire for well done.

I am doubter that the Western World has involved influenced the head of the South Sudan leaders to chase away others. The leader who wants to run the country for his interest never fought alone in liberated South Sudan from North Sudan in the first civil war. I think the definition of Democracy is to free the people from a tyrant with fair and equal right of all races. This sounds like it is not what's happening in South Sudan at this moment, because the starting of a civil war occurred between the President Salva Kiir and his reveal Vice Dr. Riek Machar. The cause the tension in a political party when the presidents Salva Kiir have sacked entire cabinet. On December 5 and 6, 2013, President Kiir called a meeting to discuss the nature of what is facing the country but did not turn out as everyone's expected to hear or see. He clearly stated, "My government never touches or you will be asking by," if you could think of Kiir who said to his opponents that I am prepared to take any action if you will try to challenge on my Presidency. Mr. Salva has blown a whistle which wake up other competitors who were busy taking a nap.

On July 8, 2016, in Juba the first Vice President Dr. Riek Machar Teny Dhurgon was called for a meeting to meet Salva Kiir, in J1, the Presidential Palace. However, the call for the meeting was a discussing between the two forces of Machar and Kiir, because the President forces have killed two Machar's bodyguard, two days before the incident. Apparently, Dr. Riek Machar thought it wasn't a big deal, earlier those morning hours. The Vice President Machar did inform his bodyguards, 75 in numbers, to go with him on a routine mission. While they were on road trip heading to J1 meeting, and Mr. Salva Kiir was busy ordering his forces to take their positions around the palace waiting for SPLM-IO to enter in the compound. After that arrived of First Vice President Dr. Machar with his bodyguards in the meeting Hall, while the meeting was in progress. The SPLA Juba opened fire to SPLM-IO while guarding Dr. Machar outside at J1 gate. And this incident was not the first thing SPLA Juba has done to SPLM-IO a week earlier gun down two of service men. The top leadership of SPLA-IO army commanders, Chief of Staff, and deputy was at Jebel. Addressing their forces compelling message, saying, "We are for peace not to fight, but today we lost two of our service men for the name reason they are Nuer, let us remind for peace." This shows only one side was committed to peace.

Who's behind the conspiracy of to assassination of Dr. Riek Machar Teny Dhurgon, in J1 in the morning hour on July 8, 2016? The plot to assassinate the first Vice President Dr. Machar had planned two weeks before he was not even left His Headquarter in Pagak. The plotters were beginning from his Camp from the two men he has trusted to do the mission of the Movement, and gave them a tremendous role in the struggle. Mastering planning to assassination plot was identified as Chief Negotiator General Taban Deng Gai. Mr. Taban was given roles as a Chief negotiator in the absence of General Pagan Amun who detained in Juba during the uprising on December 15, 2013, in state capital Juba. In fact, General Taban Deng Gai assigned in Addis Ababa, negotiation for the last two and half years in fighting. Mr. Taban has spotted by the SPLM/A-IO secret services in Juba, conducted few private meetings with Mr. Kiir, Malong, and an additional agent from the west in the closet door. The plan was that how to remove Dr. Riek from the First Vice President. The meeting was held for a good two (2) hours to execute the plans on how to make Dr.

Riek disappear from South Sudanese. Here are the final agreements made by President Kiir, Taban, Malong, and Western agent.

1. President Salva Kiir will call an emergency meeting in J1
2. Invite Dr. Riek Machar and Chief of Staff Gatwech Duel.
3. Paul Malong, make sure no one escapes when meeting start.
4. General Taban will come out as the First Vice President
5. General Taban Gai has told Kiir and Malong that he controls the opposition forces and if the plans executed happen, then all opposition units will join me.
6. In the end, they asked themselves "Do we agreed" Yes, we do.

Therefore, if you look at the news that came out first, after the Vice President had left Juba on foot to an unknown area. The two people who were on STV News making an announcement were, Makuey Lueth, the Minister of information of the government, and Taban Deng Gai, the Chief negotiator of SPLM/A- IO. General Taban Gai didn't say much to condemn the government when Mr. Makuey was saying "government is in controlled of Juba, and SPLM/A-IO has chased out from the area" General Taban, should come up with the word to defense his side. This kind of body language of General Taban has shown that is happy for his plan as he planned. To analysts of Taban plan; he was a key figure which executed all operations in the movement. No way, General Taban Gai could switch side to the government because he was the top leader who run the show during the peace process which signed to save the lives of people of South Sudan. It surprised many of South Sudanese when a news coverage came out stated that there was a fighting inside the Presidential Palace J1, the forces of Dr. Machar, and Salva Kiir. Many believe this would be the end of Dr. Riek Machar because he has no enough soldiers that could fight Fifty thousand soldiers in Juba. Fearless of 1,375 soldiers managed and protected their leader.

IGAD plus that included eight local nationals the Intergovernmental Authority on Development as well as the African Union, United Nation, EU, China, USA, UK, and Norway, who were the part of peace agent have pushed both leaders to face sanctions if not agreed. During of peace deal is Ethiopia, Dr. Riek has proposed buffer zones where both armies will leave town and stations at 25 kilometers' way. Mr. Machar was pressured by the international community to implement the peace agreement in Juba, rather than to finish it in Addis where the peace is settled. I wonder why, when the J1 incident occurred, the countries mentioned above haven't comes out to condemn the government action for attempting to assassinated opposition leader Dr. Machar. The regional leaders were well planned the plots to assassination the rebel leader. The peace that everyone's hoping to see, isnow at a dead-end, and the one thing left is fighting.

Chapter Five

DOES POLITICAL SOLUTION IS WORKING FOR SOUTH SUDAN PEOPLE?

A political solution in the Republic of the South Sudan doesn't seem to be working. I believe one would agree with me in the senseless of war and of what's going on in the Africa new nation. South Sudan has been at war by its self for three and a half years fighting while the peace agreement is pending. In African, dictator is one thing in minds of its leaders which they have been practiced for centuries and become the habit in the whole continent. African leaders have even solved their internal issue. Therefore, the only political way they solve there is to shoot your opponent in the head, clearing the pollution that could influence the general society. These mentalities we have never work in the United States of America, and the United Kingdom. Look at Africa today; people started migrating to Europe and the United States of America due to insecurity within the country. The colonialism occupation rule that was playing in Africa continent continues growing as the country is workshopping for war. Honestly, the truth must be told but not mutely, I can see from blind men of Africa who does not see the problems that are challenging them in the whole continent. Unfortunately, South Sudan situation is far from over as long as the African leaders don't think beforehand as the situation growing affects more regions. I believe will go beyond the repair if nothing done by the leaders. However, the origin of the concept of the conflict was started with the Nuer against Dinka because Nuer have been terrible slaughtered in Juba by the President which they brought to power. Now again, not only Nuer who have joined the struggle, the Equatorial, and Shilluk have been the target like the

Nuer. Back in a day when the uprising took place in Juba, people of the South Sudan have not seen the full picture of what the government turned into. The Nuer tribe were blamed because they stood up against the government which only built in the identity of ethnic line. In human ideology is in the sense of understanding the situation it comes when people face the mechanism like happened to Nuer who has massacred for no reason. Moreover, the situation which Nuer faced three years ago, and now war spreads to everywhere in the country as the government continues carrying out atrocities by killing its citizens.

I always ask myself to think more about one man whom many people become attracted to him follow and but not too long for many to drop out of his class of leadership that he may form. Dr. Riek Machar Teny Dhurgon is British-educated with a Ph.D. in Strategy planning in Bradford University the UK and later joined Sudan People Liberation Movement Army (SPLM/A) which campaign against Islamic North 1984. Dr. Riek was assigned in Upper Nile State after he was promoted to the commander to carry the attack on government forces. He was later assigned to Unity state to engaged Omer Ali Basher that later became the current President of North Sudan. On August 1991, Dr. Riek Machar decided he has not long under the leadership of Dr. John Garang, because he thought the movement was run as a family business. Dr. Riek Machar has fully announced his defection and formed his (Nasir Faction). His defection from the pivotal movement caused SPLM/A became weak in fighting Arab North because of the splitting of the army.

In six (6) years break away fighting each other, Dr. Riek Machar changed his campaign against the North, and signed peace accord call "Self-determination" with Omar Al-Bashir in 1997, and became assistant President of Omar Al-Bashir. Mr. Machar and Omar didn't get along as working. Dr. Machar quit his post as assistant to Bashir and re-launching a rebellion. In breakaway with the government was that Omar didn't commit himself to the peace that he signed. It made him change his decision to go back to the Bush to join his brothers who left in the jungle. In his return in 2002, Dr. Machar has buried what he thought that would not bring peace between him and Garang. In the agreement between Dr. Machar and Late Dr. John Garang, he became a number 3 in the SPLM/A, leadership. Mr. Machar did not disagree with structures of the Movement. After the signed peace agreement between South and North Sudan in 2005, a few days later suddenly death happened Dr. John Garang had died in Helicopter crashed which left Uganda for Sudan. After the death of Dr.

Garang, the governments have chosen Comrade Silva Kiir as the President and Dr. Machar as the Vice for the Republic of the South Sudan. Dr. Machar has done an excellent job by accepting the structure of the leadership with Dr. John Garang. If Dr. Riek Machar would have had not agreed with Dr. John Garage, for example, we would never have South Sudan as some claim as they own today. A man should earn recognition because his footprints for signing peace with Sudan as the South would remain as a separate State. Even if it never takes people long to enjoy at the same time fall back to war again. If we would have to like what Dr. John Garang was saying, "Sudan is one, and no separation army because Nubian had one battalion in the Army like the rest of Sudanese who have joined the fight too." This ideology of late Dr. John Garang would have to lead us to remain in the bush or surrender to the government of the North, or we could be like Nubian today who are campaigning against Sudan.

I believe that when someone has done an excellent job for his countrymen, then he/she would need to deserve a credit him back too. In an example, first Nyanya I, was led by Joseph Logu. And to go further more, Nyanya II formed in 1983 by Samuel Gai Tut, Abdulla Chuol Deng, and Kuot Atem these mentioned names above were the founder of Anyang II which later call Sudan People Liberation Movement Army (SPLM/A). Let us get the story right. Dr. Garang came after the movement formed. These Southern sons indeed leverage and sacrifices for the country we enjoyed and respected destroy for individual interests. We must learn to practice appreciating those who had spent their lives in the bush and done a great pronominal thing for our people. Therefore, late Dr. John Garang got to power by hijacking the movement after he went to Addis Ababa; Meet with the Ethiopia President Manigesto Alimariam. When he arrived back to Itang Wareda of Ethiopia, where the head of the movement was, Mr. Garang called a leadership emergency meeting. The downside of the meeting was to arrests Samuel Gai Tut, and Abdulla Chuol Deng. After their closed-door meeting over the phone with Manigesto. He was asking for protection forces to help him to overhaul the movement. Mr. Garang knew that Gai and Chuol Deng would not allow him leading the rebellion. And when the meeting begins, Samuel Gai suggested that, Kuot Atem will be the head of the movement. Abdulla Chuol, Garang, and he himself will go to the frontline to organize forces. Abdulla secondly Gai suggestion, but Garang disagreed with his colleagues because he already knows his strategy plan. After a few minutes, while they were on the break before going back to the meeting, Dr. Garang made calls secretly to Manigesto to rescue him immediately because he said his colleagues are planning to kill him. Mr. Manigesto had phoned the head of region 12, Governor Thokwath Pal Chay who were in charge in the area for what had happened. Governor Thokwath, his reply was, "I am aware not of what happened," immediately, Mr., Thokwath sent someone secretly to Samuel Gai, Chuol Deng, and Kuot Atem that Garang have accused you, but the President is sending enforcement to rescue Garang. Not too long after, Ethiopia troops just arrived to arrest Samuel Gai, Chuol Deng, and Kuot Atem. This blow of splits between Garang and Samuel Gai Tut ignited the fighting which led Samuel Gai and the group to chased out of the areas to Bukteng Wareda, Ethiopia where they both got killed by Garang.

Chapter Six

BIG LESSON LEARNED BUT NEVER IGNORE A SIGN

In any leadership in the world is always establish the truth, among its security organ and administration as their eyes for any activity that mutely may undergoing. Who could you trust if you don't trust your agents that could bring information to you? It's fascinating that I never heard anything in my life, the reference to what happened in Juba when Dr. Riek Machar served as Powerful Vice President in the Government of the Republic of South Sudan for eight years, and not even know his boss is trained army without knowing. President Salva Kiir had secretly recruited his common men and privately trained them not even far away from Juba in the eyes of great Vice President Dr. Machar for that long. The agents have informed the head of SPLM/A–IO leadership about the activities that are pending. In fact, Mr. Machar had ignored the real case in daylight which later became in result the loss of 26,563 Nuer in three days in the Juba in a second. One of the worst things the Dr. Machar should have admitted what he had done, as it was wrong. Furthermore, many believe because the tragedy that had occur on December 15, 2013, would never happen again as we already learned from that past. It didn't take us long again for Dr. Riek Machar to accept another risk. Going to Juba, everyone heard who was follow the news about what had happened. On July 8, 2016, when Dr. Machar and his 75 bodyguards have attacked at J1 the Presidential palace, while he was told not to go for security reasons. Dr. Riek Machar had pushed and ordered his men to prepare for the worst. Another mistake that Dr. Riek Machar had done, he should not even have accepted of 1,375 SPLM/A-IO forces to enter to Juba without grantee of trust from IGAD. The grantee trust that I would know is genuine peace is when my troops settled in buffer zone that agreed in a peace agreement, if not then I would say there is another agenda.

Mr. Kiir believe that, is Dr. Riek Machar fault when Dr. Riek says he will challenge him in coming 2018 election. In fact, we think we have democracy government that could do the right things and not change its tendency as a dictator. As a citizen of the country, any person is qualified to run for any types of senior office. Yes, you could challenge your opponents based on what you could produce. Yes, disagree with the Chairman Mr. Machar for challenging President Kiir for election. Here are a few things I think Dr. Machar could qualify him to run for Presidency: 1. The party which you affiliated would select you for party ticket. 2. What could disqualify him to run is. Dr. Machar should not challenge Salva Kiir that he will contest in upcoming 2018 election; he was a seating Vice President in the same party. But if he is out of office as Vice President, then he has a right to run for the presidency in 2018 election. Mr. Salva Kiir Mayardit knew if he leaves Dr. Machar hanging and growing seeds would produce more and would turn down his supporters. Meanwhile, the public are shouting for a regime change. He was aware that 100% Dr. Machar would win the election. President Kiir knew his strategy plan as he decided to chase away of top figures of the political leaders who could take over the leadership if people could have gone for election.

Again, we are the peace lovers, and we hope to end this conflict which displaces thousands of thousands to neighboring countries and more still trapped in UN Camps in Juba. Since day one of the Juba massacres, I always ask myself is Ban Ki-Moon the United Nation Secretary General would repatriate People out of Juba to neighbor's countries. Days go by day and look like he is going too, but nothing had happened. Is it a law in United Nation Assembly to hold people in camps in their country while people are fighting? Many of these displacement people in camps have been killed in the crossfire. So, the strategy idea for the government is to keep these people hostages in camps is for human shells. I always hear that there are human right people, who's job is to take care of individuals, but this is not what's happening now in the South Sudan. Women and girls are rapists or even killed by the government soldiers in the eyes of international community. All these UN camps that exist inside of the South Sudan have no difference then concentration Camps that used in Germany during the World War II. My people severely suffer from many things, disease, hunger, and living conditions in camps. Therefore, women have been raped every time they go out of camps during their shopping for children foods. The UN had witnessed it but had taken no action against the regime.

I remembered very well when the story was told about when the United Nations formed in San Francisco 1946. The reason for the formation of UN is to unite against countries that suppress, terrorize, and kill their people. As UN continues to build high forces, the UN charter sat in Paris, Italy in 1948 to form a Human right watch and again in Geneva in 1949 to have a declaration of Convention to discuss such issues that happen around the world, for example, South Sudan and in Rwanda. The same topic we need to remind ourselves of past events. History keeps us in loops in things we have experience in the past. I wonder if the UN has forgotten its role in the world, taking care of human lives. In 1994 in Rwanda, there were major massacres between Tutsi and Hutu, these killings have shocked the world, immediately UN stepped in arresting the top figures who behind the massacre and brought to world Criminal Tribunal. If UN is still on that roles bringing Criminals to Justice like what happened to Rwanda 1994, and UN should have still done that in the South Sudan. President Kiir and those who committed massacres would have to bring to World Criminal Tribunal Court to face their actions against humanity. There no doubt about the killings because it happened in front of the international watch, but is not what is going on now South Sudan. The IGAD, UN, AU, UK, U.S., and Norway are for the government.

If you do not want tyranny, malice, murders or genocide to happen to people in your or our homes, then YOU must act to stop this. Let us all put something in motion to prevent these terrible things from happening. I believe to be successful in ending this struggle then you can't be scared to die for the truth. The fact is that these things are happening in South Sudan, as they occurred in Rwanda over 25 years ago. Know the truth about the struggles of the people in South Sudan and doing something about it is the only thing that is ever going to save lives. And it is human lives that are at risk here. Women, children dying for no reason at all! Please, I encourage you to do something about these issues and not to give up hope to save the people of South Sudan. But if you quit or do not do something about it, the killing of innocents will continue to happen. This regime would pursue and last forever if nothing were ever done!

Chapter Seven

NEVER MIND DO YOURS, AND I DO MIND

The one snare tribe in South Sudan that calls themselves Jeng Council of Elders (JCE) and this name has been a center of Cliff show in South Sudan's politics as many tribes were angry for the coming of the name. I believe or creation a name is not an issue that could bring more nicotine in our country because of whatever is going on. Roughly, sleeping being not stand by, which one would be your first choice as I referred to above mention the name. *Stay awake* means a lot to individuals who mean business because it would push them to the next level controlling while others are busy. To point a finger to someone because they created a group name. Blame would never convince their attitude to stop because you encourage them to do more harms. If I were you, you would do the same thing because know you come from a tribe that have elders that have great ideas like Jeng Council of Elders. Any person or leader must come from their tribe, and if tribes become unorganized, then it would not be other problems. To correct what said all the time. For example, Nuer, Shilluk, and rest of the South Sudan tribes are sleeping while Dinka community is on stage weighing war against other tribes. Nuer were preventing by whom saying do not organize, isn't their weakness. I believe in the bottom of my heart that is not too late to do just that.

Why do people choose him as to lead the rebellion against the government? And this not the first time to lead a Movement. I believe his choice to lead this movement was not his intention as a job he interested to do. Dr. Machar is a man with defensive difference ideology of belief, no one would know what he wants. I mean when a leader decided rebellion within ranks of the same movement or government. The two things would happen. 1. As a defector, your life will be at risk because the other group will hunt you down. 2. Act quickly to organize forces to become ready fully for your objective. In my mind, I believe that Dr. Machar is willing to accept a political solution so that people could go back on the table again. Mr. Kiir is not ready for peace; the government was on defensive since they signed a memorandum of ceasefire in January of 2014, until these days. When a dictator knew his plans, he always executes his plan for good until the end. Salva Kiir is not ready to lower his bar down because he has gained support from Regional Blocs, such as Uganda, Kenya, and Ethiopia. If I mistake, why these countries leaders have not done the right thing to force Salva Kiir for what he was doing violated ceasefire that was signed. The world is affiliates of no truth, so leaders have filled with lies that killed real numbers of a human. Is God is watching what is going on in the third world country? If you look at Africa, is a place where the US, U.K., and China conduct the very worst business involves dragging African sons and daughters to fight each other. I believe that African leaders will never see the Western World's influence over Africa continent. Africa has many resources, same likes any other first world countries has, it's the first continent that has a lots problem. An example, war, and diseases have dominated entire Africa.

Chapter Eight

WHAT IF AFRICAN LEADERS TODAY COULD HAVE ACCEPTED THE IDEAS OF UNITED STATE OF AFRICA?

PAN African was found in 1963 when the continent of Africa most its countries were under colonies rules, but some gained their independence. The thirty-three African leaders met in Addis Ababa, on May 24, 1963. The agenda for the meeting was to form Africa as United Africa with one Passport, one army, one President. Only a few leaders were agreed to support Kwame Nkrumah, Julius Nyerere, Haile Selassie, Jomo Kenyatta but much of them opposed the mention heads of state. Moreover, because white settlers who were physically present and saw where African leaders led, they continue still controlled mentality of these leaders. Africa would have been a peaceful country if the idea had frequently passed with no double agents minded.

Shortly not too long after, the uprising began melting overthrows leaders who might have opposed white's settlers. Julius Nyerere, Haile Selassie, and Kwame Nkrumah have overthrown because of their ideas they had presented to the Africa Union in 1963. If you can look at Africa, is not run by leaders independently but it run by first world leaders. Again, what African doesn't have regarding endearment, love, and emperor, like others? Africans have many resources: wildlife, oil, and you can name it. What good mind does African people doesn't have then any others human on earth? God created every human being equal with the same thinking, but one chooses to allow others to think for them. Of course, America has the greatest thing helping country financially, foods, and medical. Honestly, I'm not in denial, the assistance by the

United States is appreciated. My point is if U.S. is continues helping countries financially, while there is no change among the countries then there will be no use of the government to exist. These countries that U.S. is helping them have same resources as America.

Chapter Nine

CORRECT ME OR AGREE WITH THE FACT THE ABOUT SOUTH SUDAN MISLEADING LEADERS

South Sudan is a strange country with leaders that are pretending to do the right thing, but indeed they are not. See what had happened and is still happening these days. If a leader observes and knows his failure, he should not take long to recover what he had undermined for so long. And if one continues not to consider a concern for what is happening to the country. The ruining of your legacy not knowing while leading nation will also come back in history as a failed leader. During the South Sudan referendum on July 9, 2011, the people voted President Salva Kiir as their leader of 99% voted. I trust South Sudan citizens who have been put their trust on President Kiir, but it turned out that people have elected Hyena to take care of goats, and now people are becoming wonder. First lesson, but let us not select a corrupt leader to care of us next time because if people knew in the first place, then people would never make that messy choice. In fact, it's crucial for South Sudan leadership to invest their personal interest than to recover a country from tearing apart.

I wonder if corruption and tribalism are ones destroyed the image of a great nation. In my mind, there no question that one could say more than this because of behavior allowed by the leaders, South would have still shouting for joy, and share values together like when they fought Arab together with one common purpose. Corruption is one of severe untreated fever in the world, and add up with tribalism together then it becomes deadly disease we see today. What happened in Juba on that day when thousands of Nuer were massacred if it wasn't tribalism. I can understand why President Salva Kiir is frustrated in his leadership is because he consumed all the country resources and points finger to others. Therefore, the killings of innocent people in Juba who have nothing to do with politics cause more concern as a regime is practicing a dictator mind which cause people to wonder.

Chapter Ten

THE UNITED NATION ROLE IN THE WORLD CONFLICTS

I remembered very well when the story was told about when the United Nations formed in San Francisco 1946. The reason for the formation of UN is to unite against a country that will act and committed killings of its people. Leaders sat agreed on the UN shatter. As UN continues to build high forces, the UN charter sat in Paris, Italy in 1948 to form a Human right watch and again in Geneva in 1949 to have a declaration of Convention. The same issue we need to remind ourselves of past events. History keeps us in loops in things we have experience in the past. I wonder if the UN has forgotten its role in the world, taking care of human lives. In 1994 in Rwanda, there were major massacres between Tutsi and Hutu, these killings have shocked the world, immediately UN stepped in arresting the top figures who behind the massacre and brought to world Criminal Tribunal. If the UN is still one that roles bringing Criminals to Justice like what happened to Rwanda 1994, and UN should have still done that in the South Sudan. President Kiir and those who committed massacres would have to bring to World Criminal Tribunal Court to face their actions against humanity. There no doubt about the killings because it happened in front of the international watch, but is not what is going on now South Sudan. The IGAD, UN, AU, UK, U.S., and Norway are for the government.

Another role United Nation should play in South Sudan conflict is the protection of displacement people who stripped in UN Camps in Juba. Also, one thing UN had shown is to add additional forces in United Nation Mission for South Sudan Camps. But it's not a solution to end the conflict by adding more troops to present in South Sudan. One best thing is bringing President Salva Kiir regime to face Justice for their actions which because thousands lives in three days. The general public is tired of this government exists on this planet. Anything is possible tomorrow if rebels take over the country, then neighbors' countries who for the government one day will rush to congratulate the new leadership and build relationships. It's not too long for happening, but I can see the real change is near and as many people stand up together to fight the corrupt regime. Moreover, in Equatorial states, the government is carrying the same killing of what they did in Juba and elsewhere in South Sudan. If even hanging on power for this short this period, still not going to take them long.

Chapter Eleven

NGUNDENG BONG'S PROPHECIES ARE REAL

Don't take me wrong, we are all human and we cannot be perfect, accept Jesus the Son of God who was born free from our sins. But every human was against him during his time in 13 AD. Some of us today may say, "I was not the part of those who revolted against the man son of God, but we sinned through Adam and Eve's blood. The point that I want to make is that no prophets can be trusted by his people unless by the full community. Even the prophet Ngundeng himself his prophecies have been preached to many people of South Sudanese tribes. Gok Ngundeng Bong have been preaching his words about things that would happen to people of the Sudan. In fact, Prophet Ngundeng or (give from God) did, in fact, mention couple's names during his prophecies and thing that will happen. I have many scholars' articles criticizing Ngundeng Bong his words that he has said to people lives around Wech Deng of Lou Nuer of Akobo in the State of Jonglei. I think those scholars who have studied him have not understood Prophet Ngundeng Bong well. It is always good to learn that language to understand the barrier of that tribe as you do your research finding story tale.

In the Bible Matthew 24:6 Jesus said, "And you shall hear of wars and rumors of wars: see that you are not troubled: for all these things, must come to pass, but the end is not yet" I think Jesus is right, we see wars and Nation against the nation. If you look at Ngundeng and traces back his prophecies about things he mentioned such as ten states (Wee Wal), my flag will not add with Jalaba which mean separation from the Arab North. He mentions Garang,

Kiir Nyalanydieng. Garang will lead for 21 years, but those 21 years will be 21 days. Yes, that happened, John Garang led the rebellion for those years as he mentioned. After he signed the peace agreement with Sudan, after 21 days' peace accord, Garang has died in plans crush. Even Prophet Ngundeng Bong said,"You will hear Garang like earring," these are concrete facts that many believe had happened and continues occurring.

Don't quote me wrong because I have compared Jesus's prophetic about his return to earth. We know Jesus Christ is a son of God, but some individuals may react that way by saying why the writer compares Jesus to Ngundeng. Honestly, I'm trying to make a point because only a few people in this world believe Jesus will return, but the majority did not agree with the Bible. Yes, hundred percent believe Jesus will come back per the Bible mentioned.

The Vice President Dr. Riek Machar did not seek a change of the government for his political interests, but he has to speak on behalf of the people because if you look at innocent people in many states. No developments, the government is not interested in delivering services to the people, so someone has to speak for them if no one stood up. Dr. Riek is a man that is gaining more followers not only in their respective tribe but everywhere in South Sudan. This doleful of sorrow would not wash away unless one man stands to rescue the public. The very first people who liberated the people from Arab North must admire for their full participation in fighting for whole South Sudan. Someone should do the same channel, if not people will remain dictator regime for life. Africa leaders have practiced this kind of sensor for centuries, so people must organize as one people to fight injustice to be free.

Chapter Twelve

A FOLLOWER SOMETIMES BECOMES A LEADER

The South Sudan political crisis is more like ammunition that was spreading all over when you try to collect them while the enemy is approaching. But in human history come with humanity when the people of this world start to think to conquer another person like them, these kinds of beliefs which created lots of distracting aligning of what it's today. For leaders who happen not to fear of his/her followers, so their supporters rapidly grow and gains much more support bigger than ever. Indeed, but for the leader which fear and look suspicious to their supporters than his leadership fall like dropping objects from the sky. To grow the best seeds are essential ambivalence attitude which could attract many people to be part of the direction and become alternate after leaving the stage ever. I believe the great leader produce seeds that can multiply mores which make the leader style of being adapting by those who you have trained for that work under your style, people would watch you do, and become stylish coping your work along with the same kind of work you do. Thus, many leaders are willing merely to produce followers, expecting new leaders to show up on the scene when their time comes. Those types of leaders have no idea how much they are limiting their potential and the potential of the people around them.

As I have said before, a leader who produces followers defines his success to what his direct, person influence touches. His success ends when he can no longer lead. On the other hand, a leader who produces other leaders multiplies his power, and he and his people have a future. So, his leadership continues to build and grow even if he is personally unable to carry on his leadership role. I believe that the leader must be an agent that could change environmental. Yes, it's true a leader could change the government system which gives him/her credibility as someone who cares about its people.

Chapter Thirteen

DO AFRICAN LEADERS THINK ENOUGH TO FIX THE SOUTH SUDAN PROBLEM?
On November 19, 2016, in Addis Ababa at Bole International Airport of Ethiopia, SPLM-IO Chairman Dr. Riek Machar Teny, left South Africa after treatment heading for Pagak Headquarter of the Movement. Dr. Machar was boarding the flight to Khartoum, Sudan and Addis Ababa, Ethiopia. On his arrival at the gate in Khartoum Airport, Dr. Machar held by the security agents not allowed to exit until he contacted the President of the Sudan Omer Ali Bashier. The Sudan President did of course denial Mr. Machar to the entrance to the city, which made him head for Addis where he was also denial by Ethiopia Prime Ministry Dessalem Alimiriam. Dr. Riek Machar was in fact detained at Bole Airport for few hours until the Prime Ministry allowing him to stay in the city overnight and the next day Mr. Machar head back to South Africa until further notice from Ethiopia Authority. Two months earlier U.S. Secretary of the States John Karry had a short visit in Kenya. His visit to Kenya was to convince East African leaders to support Kiir's regime and isolate South Sudan rebel leader Dr. Riek Machar.

The purpose of the meeting was to place warrant arrest on rebel leader and top military commanders in the army. It didn't take long then the Press Secretary of the SPLM-IO Movement James Gatdet Dak Lampuor was arrested in his compound in Nairobi Kenya at 5 pm by the Kenya security and that morning he back to the government of Kiir. The Kenya authority had handed James Gatdet Dak over to the national security of Juba, where he was interrogated and brutally beaten. The U.S. Secretary of States is brutal to destroy

African leaders who have the vision to the country to bring real change to its people. The absence or restriction of Dr. Riek to out of the Republic of South Sudan will not help the situation to calm. The aboriginal language that is used by John Karry of U.S. to influence East Africa Countries will not silence the roaring guns. It will continue to bring more distress because Dr. Machar is a leader who goal is full in living peace. I believe it that pull him aside will allowing the general population is joining the Resistance Movement to toupees the regime as possible.

African leaders would even never be accomplishing anything over the South Sudan peace because African has their internal problem in which they couldn't solve the problem in South Sudan. The countries, such as Uganda, Kenya, and Ethiopia have come to resolve internal issues which are looming security concerns in the country. Politely believe that no patient would feed another rather than seeking for treatment to cure the sickness. This compelling way of IGAD peace strategy planning was sunk evidently in their internal problems which are the reason they shouldn't do the order right. The winning of the war without potential ability of quidding principle, a leader would be like an animal that fell in a pit fighting out for their life. Merely, IGAD region leaders potentially on encouraging Mr. Master killer Kiir, but doesn't realized that the citizens are abundant the country for neighbor's country.

Chapter Fourteen

OPEN THE NEW CHAPTER

After waiting for a few months since the J1 Palace incident. The SPLM/IO supporters are wrestling for reconstruction of its leadership after the defections of most top SPLM-IO leaders to the government of Kiir. On December 2, 2016, in South Africa, Dr. Machar has appointed Henry Odwar as the Deputy of the Chairman of the Army Movement and Honorable Stephen Par Kuol as Foreign relations and external affairs. It's a hectic decision that the Chairman of the Movement has made in the last five months as the chief negotiator of the movement Taban Deng Gai betrayed the Resistance Movement and switched side to the regime. The Chairman appointed the new face of leadership, replacing the double standing agents who betrayed its people. The speeding will quickly process the Army struggle to tight up the government quicker as possible.

If you want to be successful as bad as you want to be within the struggle, remember that uprising takes many lives. It's not time, and can't be afraid to die in the truth, and it's the only thing that ever free you from that hold hostage. The end of pain is success, which you are not going to die because you feel the little fever. Many people have lost their loved ones, but don't have to cry to give up, they cry to keep going. Don't cry to give up, you're already hurt from it from the government. This is not the time to go to sleep until you get rid of the government. As you know how the saying goes, pain is temporary that could last for the hour, minutes, and even a year but even actually, it subsides, but if you give up, however, will last forever.

Chapter Fifteen

UNKNOWN GUNMEN IN JUBA

Fascinating vogue word, which the Republic of South Sudan has called, "unknown gunmen", these unknown militants are on social media before the independence of the South Sudan. Why would I mislead my people if I knew I'm in charge of the country? It could take me a minute to find who's the unknown gunmen, if I do know, hundreds of percent believe l' m in control of the security organs army, police, private security, and secret service. The word "unknown gunmen" is alarming the people because the president is not in control of the country if the gunmen created an uprising in the country. I don't think the president is telling adequate reason to speak the fact about what caused all but to blind other not too.

In 12 years of unknown shooters, debutant acts of killing, which caused these events as a regime, is always said when they do a news conference. Especially, December 15, 2013, of presidential guards of Tiger Battalion at Jebel, July 8, 2016, and the Presidential Palace of J1. The government comes out with the name they do not wish to take responsible for criminal activity even they knew them. The criminal always has so many mean to get out the situation. Even though the criminal who had been found guilty, he would still insist not to accept what he has been changed with. Same to atrocious, horrible killings that have taken place in Juba, the government would have never admitted as a somewhat happened they did. In doing what so ever, the people they lead will take note on how they horribly lie to people who put them in power. Lair sometimes helps for once not repeatedly, but citizens could become a wonder for a leader who doesn't accept their responsibility for what happened in the country.

Chapter Sixteen

COUP PLOT WITHIN SPLM-IO ITSELF AT CROWN HOTEL JUBA

Coup plot has plans in Crown Hotel in Juba by the two gentlemen namely, Taban Deng Gai and Ezekiel Lol Gatkuoth. Mr. Taban has on radar by SPLM-IO security agents, but the leadership has kept ignoring the sign of their moves. Until the last minutes when he knew that the chairman of the movement had pushed out of the State capital by the President Kiir's, forces pursued them all the way to the Congo for thirty-seven days (37) until government troops exhausted, fighting fearless Dr. Machar forces. History doesn't make itself but instead is made by human beings. However, Dr. Machar hasn't done anything wrong in term of putting his truth on the Juba Crown Hotel coup plotter of Taban Deng Gai, and Ezekiel Lol Gatkuoth.

Truth with promise is no longer working as the two men changed their strategies and switched sides by joining the man they said, "Murdered 26, 000 Nuer in Juba". The interesting part of Mr. Taban and Lol Gatkuoth motive roles is to change their culture because not interesting in the bush. Nerveless, it's a tradition in the South Sudan politics, to switch a side, even with the numbers deaths among them.

Chapter Seventeen

SOUTH SUDAN IS ALREADY A FAIL COUNTRY

As highlighted before, it's very clear that South Sudan problem are not a quick fix among the political elites. They are not interested in bringing their differences to the table to recover citizens that are dying. A real leader is not concerned with the opinions of others, but with getting a job done and working towards a common goal. Many people are always happy enough to take the credit for having been right, in fact, few are willing to take the blame for having been wrong. I believe in my mind that the wise leader is always more concerned with what's than with the way he/she would want things to be. Therefore, he's concerned with what will work than with getting his mere opinions accepted. A wisely leader is not afraid of submitting his ideas to the test of reality. It is a sign of weakness in a leader for him to pull rank with the argument. Alternatively, if a leader fails to win popularity by this mean, he would have to do well to find a way to compromise or even to suggest maybe some other solution that the people will be able to understand and accept as reasonable. But Mr. Kiir is only busy shopping and selling country resources such as oil to countries that could supply them with guns to the general population of South Sudan. Over 3 million population already left the country to neighboring countries. A leader who knows the reality would have to think twice of reading people's minds as to why they leave the country.

Chapter Eighteen

DOES NATIONAL PRAYER OF SALVER KIIR MEAN ANYTHING?

Killer of the people always on moves not going to sleep but could calm the people for to have pay attention about things that may be happening. President Kiir does it to let the people not aware of the situation of the country. He has created the public prayer so that he can order his armies to commit some killing for the last three year of fighting. Arresting people who flee to neighboring countries, such as Uganda, Kenya, and Ethiopia. The citizens of the South Sudan have much distrust of Mr. Kiir and his shoes shined. The South Sudan situation will never be solved by the African leaders who call themselves (IGAD) because they declared their support on the government side. In many cases when leaders involved addressing the problem may sometimes announce its support, that peace always would never as people would expect. This excellent example could see in the South Sudan as IGAD (REGION) leaders played significant roles, squeezed SPLM-IO leaders and supporters, arrested them for deporting to Juba. Imagine that if one sees such a move from IGAD leaders, a wave of peace that people are hoping to see is dismantled as region leaders have looked to the shadow side of peace. Many of you may agree with the point that I have made about African leaders who have never acknowledged their problems, which are always waiting for those leaders from the West to give them directives on how to do their works.

Therefore, many tribes in South Sudan that are facing this war that includes Kiir's tribes, have already learned much about dictator life, starting when he first took the oath as the President of the Republic of South Sudan.

Promising the people that he will do everything based on the law of the nation. The road to election, build institutions such as educations, and Hospitals delivering services to the people of the great country. Those promises hadn't happened.

Talking over of the leadership of Salver Kiir, because you shouldn't be talking first for no plan ahead, in reality it need true complement among the people of the country. In this talk, we have seen it in our own eyes, our country situation needs our attention because it could end. At the beginning of the war, which was started on the Nuer tribe, which were killed in Juba, nation capital. The rest of the tribes saw it was the Nuer problem, but today it happened that it wasn't a Nuer issue alone. Seeing and hearing have difference instincts, now Kiir is still killing the people of South Sudan. Therefore, international community has channeled their truth to the government. There is something other countries are interested in, specially, Uganda, Ethiopia, Kenya, AU, IGAD, U.S. UK, they said that if leader is being opposed by the Nuer tribe that he kills on December 15, 2013, now they are returning to President Salver Kiir who kills them. If they were killed, we don't think they could go back the man who slaughtered them like animals; innocent's women, men, kids, unborn child, preachers, and teachers. If you could look at it this, you would think it can't be true because people keep going back to someone who committed that killing as all world saw. And this show that you don't know your own problem.

Secondly, the person who oversaw peace, and we put our truth on him, has a private discussion between him and Mr. Kiir, that wasn't shown to SPLM/A-IO leadership when he was in bush as the chief negotiator for peace. Therefore, when he knew the chairman has arrived in Juba, he planned the way to assassinated Dr. Riek Machar. Mr. Taban has told his comrades that the place where a Dr. Riek could have to assassinate is a meeting place, because he will come with small numbers of body guards. General Taban secretly has told this to those who believe him the strategies plan to kill Mr. Machar.

For that reason, the international community has placed their truth to Nuer like another world. Therefore, they were saying Taban is Nuer by tribe before he was talking in defending his Movement during the peace agreement. And Taban was so tough in responses of Nuer killing, before he switched sides by joining Salver Kiir, who he did classify as a killer and became best friends. But left leaving people unbelieving of what he had done to his community. Losing love with the community you belong to is always a huge setback and hard to regain when nothing happens.

Chapter Nineteen

KIIR, TABAN, AND MALONG THEIR PLAN ARE WORKING.

One reason why those names mentioned above is that they are the master planner in South Sudan's ignited fire which created thousands kills and million people displaced out of the country. Today, the government has detained rebel leader Dr. Riek Machar in South Africa. He cannot travel anywhere, even Pagak the headquarter. The world leaders have ruled out their supports to a regime and the signed of the peace is became nothing. The signatory's leaders, who have witness what have been signed in Addis Ababa, Ethiopia, should not waste time as they could not rule to side with Salva Kiir.

The rebel committed to true peace, that it signed during agreement in Ethiopia Capital Addis Ababa, as rebel remains on their position based on peace regulation like violation of peace, such as attack on other. However, in respect of the peace to save the people of South Sudan, the government went on offensive, carrying many attacks to control areas the where controlled by Opposition group. The Ten (10) cities in the areas of Opposition were captured on purpose of SPLM/A-IO, is believed, in peace, to save lives. The regime is really focused on gaining more territories that are being control by the rebels. The opposition has lost some keys strategy towns, such as Nasir, Doleib Hill, Waat, Yuei, Owaci, Kodok, and Wau Shilluk, Kuek, and many more. Meanwhile, many thought peace is there for two warring parties to cool down heat that burning people alive.

Upset among the supporters is an urgent need that a leader should deal with when people become unaware of how the movement is being run. The supporters want rebels to speed up their fighting with the government. A huge thing that civilians don't know is that rebel and regime were asked by the U.S., UK., and IGAD to accept peace. Any group that would refuse to cooperate with this request would then be replaced under United Nation suction.

Being a rebel, is not always easy in the world community. It takes time for people to understand the position of the rebel, why they choose to fight, and to discuss their needs with the government. The regime in Juba force, the people fight them because obtaining hostages violated the right of the people of South Sudan. Sometimes, leaders must hear the world body, who plays the most important roles in world conflicts.

It's important for people of the Republic of South Sudan to express their feelings, concerns and effective changes that would also bring better life to others. The world of today wants you to speak up before they can help recuse people from a tyrant government. The tyrant regime has turned the country into a graveyard as it continues committing crime against humanity.

In May 2017, the mediators of IGAD, U.K., U.S. and plus AU have urged the worried parties to call for sustainable peace reconciliation again in Addis Ababa, Ethiopia. Hello, comrades, the 2016 peace agreement which led the opposition leadership to land in Juba was the honorable peace which a country could have. 1. Opposition armed group led by First Vice President had committed to peace without anything left out. 2. Top leadership of Opposition had touched down in the state Capital with small soldiers with no others plans in concern if something does break up. 3. During Addis Ababa peace agreement, SPLM/A-IO have decided to save the life's innocent people who have been facing hard life in the region. The opposition group have dismissed war and put the people first on their commons goals. On the other hand, Salva haven't had ever dreamt about the people life, as many are dying of gun wound, hungry, and living conditions in the country it's an absolutely fact.

CHAPTER TWENTY

IT'S FOUR YEARS SINCE JUBA'S MASSECRED

Four years since the Juba massacred, the African leaders and other world leaders have kept silence on South Sudan's civil war. The core principle politics for the world leaders are to support a country which they have a relationship with, but it doesn't matter if people are killed or not. Recently, the mediators of peace process have called the rebel Headquarter of Pagak, and Juba regime for immediate ceasefire.

The calls came after the meeting of the mediators, but sound like a juke when people of South Sudan heard it because no one would ever believe such some quick moves urging rebel leader and the president to wrap up for true peace. I'm not so sure if the peace monitor groups have ever ascended, looking over the agreed agenda during the peace period. Although, if they do then it would be peace mediators to yield to direction of President Kiir to militarize Juba into zones, a lest 25 miles from Juba town. If we meant the real peace in the country, would be a peace when the personal interests do not allow to appear on parties negotiating table.

Impeccable National Dialogues which was started on May 21, 2017, in Juba. The National Dialogues was attended by Juba regime and greet distressful people who happen to have no say anymore. The dialogue which is Juba government call it "National Dialogue" would not even affect or changes the minds of those in the bush to turn themselves in. It's the way of the Juba, to propagated their moves to calm the situation not to make an attack on the opposition. It had occurred on different occasions, one time they had called for National Prayer in the country, which became murdered month ever. As Equatorial people have been rounded up in their family home's, burned alive.

Another situation about which everyone's alarmed, is National Dialogue. The Juba regime has created these acts to confuse the situation. The concept of dialogue, to which they used to make peace with no army. The problem are even more difficult because the active army group that fight the government today was not even invited. How a national dialogue could work without opposition be involved, if Mr. Kiir wants to save lives. It is a surprise move by Juba regime on a light platform to end the war. Although, having a blessing of peace in South Sudan, people must go back to August 26, 2015, which was signed by the President and first Vice President. There will never be a fruitful peace than that of August of 2015, which led the Pagak leadership to take the first trip to Juba and to implement the peace accord.

www.ingramcontent.com/pod-product-compliance
Lightning Source LLC
Chambersburg PA
CBHW050758240726
48654CB00008B/545